WE NEED TO [TALK] ABOUT
VAGINAS

NEON SQUID

CONTENTS

INTRODUCTION

Dear vagina owner—this book is for you!

As a mom of girls and a **gynecologist** (a doctor who specializes in the female reproductive system), I find that my daughters' friends love asking me questions about their bodies, vaginas, and vulvas. They want to understand if their experiences are normal. I realized that many young people have very few places to turn to when they need information. Their friends are often just as **in the dark** about their bodies as they are!

Books about bodies often talk about biology and science. We will do that in this book, but I also want you to understand the normal parts of **growing and changing**, and how they affect your daily life.

This is a book for you to read as you explore how your body works and how it is changing as you grow from a child to a teenager to an adult.

I want to share an inclusive and **body-positive** view of loving yourself and understanding how your body works. You own your body! You deserve to understand it so you can be **empowered** to make decisions about how to take care of it.

You may have questions that are personal and private, and you may not know where to go for the answers or who to ask. Hopefully this book will help answer many of those questions, but if not, turning to reliable sources is important. Not everyone on the internet and social media has **accurate information**.

Some of the topics in this book may make you feel a little uncomfortable. That's OK! It's good to think about tricky issues, even if they make you feel a little awkward. Not all of the topics may relate to you, but understanding what others are going through is important too.

So, let's talk about vaginas!

Dr. Allison K. Rodgers

FEMALE BODIES

In **different cultures** and throughout time, there have been different attitudes about vaginas, female-gendered bodies, and sexuality. Why do some people think that talking and learning about female bodies and how they work is inappropriate? Well, what is "inappropriate" is really a **social construct**, meaning that every culture determines what is OK and not OK to talk about. Some people may think this very book is inappropriate! The truth is that you deserve to **understand your body**, but it's also important to understand why other people feel the way they do.

OPEN DISCUSSIONS

You need to know about your body in order to understand how to take care of it. Learning in school, from a doctor, or from a trusted adult in your life is often the best way to get information.

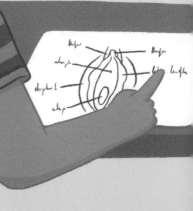

PROTESTS

Female health and sexuality is often the topic of protests. Protests allow people to express their feelings and challenge their society, culture, and government to consider other views about sensitive topics.

J. MARION SIMS

Nicknamed the "father of modern gynecology," J. Marion Sims advanced much of our understanding about female reproductive health. He developed many surgical instruments we still use today. However, Sims experimented on Black enslaved people in the United States in the 1840s. These women didn't have a choice and were not given pain medication because of a racist notion that Black people did not feel pain. It's important to understand where our knowledge comes from.

FEMALE GENITAL MUTILATION

In many parts of the world, a tradition called female genital mutilation (FGM) is common practice. During FGM the external genitals of a girl or woman are removed, for religious or cultural reasons. This practice has no health benefits; in fact, it can cause infection, permanent disfigurement, and harm. It can also make future childbirth dangerous for both the mother and the baby. FGM is banned in lots of countries.

MORE THAN 200 MILLION PEOPLE ALIVE TODAY HAVE UNDERGONE FGM.

Source: UNICEF

MYTHS AND HISTORY

In ancient times, before people understood how childbirth worked, there were lots of different ideas and myths about the role of the **womb** (uterus) and **vagina**. The ability of a womb to create life has been seen as powerful and magical in many different cultures and civilizations throughout the world. Before scientists discovered how our bodies work, many of these myths were accepted as facts—and some still are.

THE FLYING VAGINA

One ancient Hawaiian myth describes the fertility goddess Kapo, who had a detachable flying vagina! Kapo saved her sister, who was being attacked by a dangerous pig god, by sending her flying vagina to lure him away. It crashed into the ground, causing a giant crater that trapped the pig god.

WANDERING WOMB

In ancient Greece, the uterus was thought to travel around the body causing problems wherever it went. If you had a headache, they believed it was because your uterus had wandered up to your head! The ancient Greeks also believed the uterus caused women to act crazily, hence the term hysteria (*hystera* is the Greek word for womb).

SHEELA NA GIGS

These ancient carvings depict naked women with enlarged vulvas (the outer parts of a female's genitals, or private parts). They are found carved on buildings and churches in Europe and date back to the 11th century.

PREHISTORIC FIGURES

Carvings of the female figure have been found from the earliest civilizations. They are typically small and depict exaggerated body curves. What need would ancient people have for these figures? Some historians think it could be related to religion or trying to improve fertility.

9

GETTING TO KNOW
YOUR VULVA

The word *vulva* refers to all of the **outside parts** of your genitals, or private parts. Lots of people call these bits your vagina, but that's not correct! It's important to know the different parts of your body so you can take care of yourself and stay healthy. Understand what your vulva **normally looks like**, so if something changes, you will notice it. No one should understand your body better than you!

USE A MIRROR!

It's nearly impossible to see your vulva without the help of a mirror. Sit on the floor or bed with your heels together and knees spread to the sides. Place the mirror near your heels, and adjust the angle until you are able to see everything clearly.

It takes some practice to hold the mirror to see down there.

MAKE SURE YOU ARE SOMEWHERE **SAFE** AND **PRIVATE** BEFORE LOOKING AT YOUR VULVA.

WHAT'S IT ALL CALLED?

If you have a vulva, try to identify the different parts on your own body. People often misuse the word *vagina*. The vagina is only the inside canal between the outside of your body and the cervix, which is part of the uterus. The rest is the vulva!

Mons pubis: the small, fatty pad with pubic hair that sits on top of the pubic bone.

Clitoris: a sensitive nerve bundle that gives a pleasure sensation.

Labia minora: the inner lips of the vulva have very delicate skin.

Urethra: the opening where pee (urine) comes out from the bladder.

Labia majora: the outer lips of the vulva where pubic hair grows.

Vaginal opening: the outside, or start, of the vaginal canal. Also known as the introitus.

Perineum: the delicate skin between the vulva and the anus.

Anus: this opening is where poop leaves the body.

WHAT'S GOING ON IN THERE?

Before we get started, it's important to know exactly what we're talking about when we're discussing what goes on "down there." There are lots of nicknames for female reproductive parts, but in this book we'll be dealing with the proper names! Your reproductive organs live in the **middle of your pelvis** between your bladder (where pee comes from) and rectum (where poop comes from). The uterus is an **amazing organ**. It starts off the size of your fist, but it can grow to the size of a watermelon when a baby is inside it, before going back to the size of your fist again! Let's take a closer look.

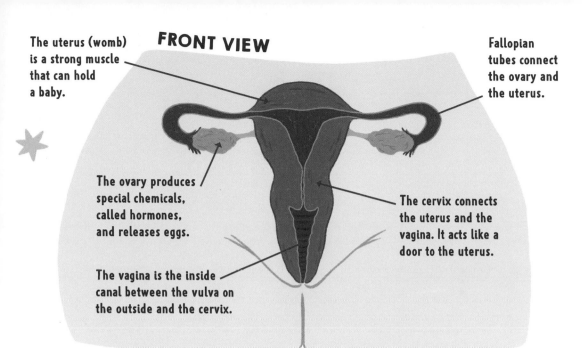

FRONT VIEW

The uterus (womb) is a strong muscle that can hold a baby.

Fallopian tubes connect the ovary and the uterus.

The ovary produces special chemicals, called hormones, and releases eggs.

The cervix connects the uterus and the vagina. It acts like a door to the uterus.

The vagina is the inside canal between the vulva on the outside and the cervix.

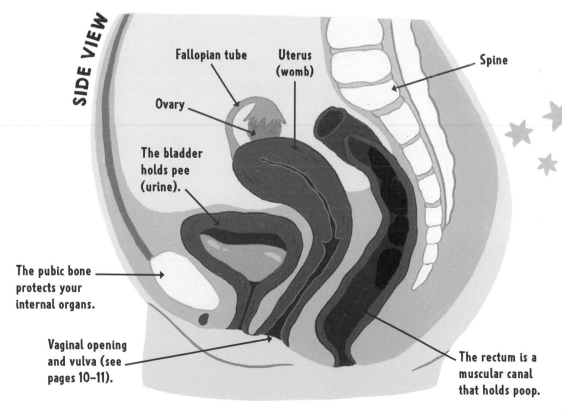

SIDE VIEW

Fallopian tube

Uterus (womb)

Spine

Ovary

The bladder holds pee (urine).

The pubic bone protects your internal organs.

Vaginal opening and vulva (see pages 10–11).

The rectum is a muscular canal that holds poop.

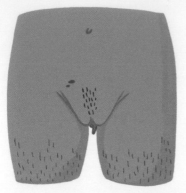

One side may be **different** than the other.

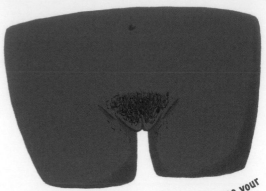

You may not be able to see your labia minora from the **outside**.

EVERYONE'S
DIFFERENT

Just like snowflakes and fingerprints, each vulva is unique—no two are the same! The vulva and labia change and grow during **puberty**, the period when children start to turn into adults (see pages 16–17). It's normal for everyone's labia to look different. Labia minora (the inner lips) are very sensitive, and if they are longer or hang down, they may rub on your clothes. **Pubic hair** does a great job of protecting them by creating a helpful cushion!

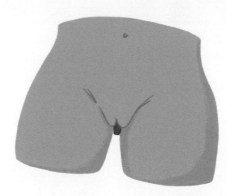

The labia minora can be **longer** and **larger** than the labia majora.

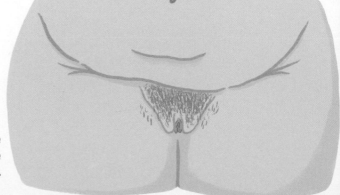

Sometimes the labia minora are **just visible**.

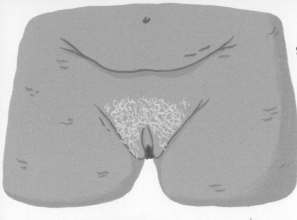

Some labia are **smooth** and some are **wrinkly**.

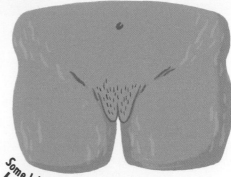

Labia majora can be **bigger** than labia minora.

Some labia can **hang down**.

Labia majora can be **puffy** or they can lie more flat to the body.

BODY IMAGE

How you feel about your body is important. Bodies that you see in magazines or on TV are often fake and can lead to unrealistic expectations of what you should look like. Negative feelings about your size, shape, or appearance are dangerous to your self-esteem.

Puberty is the process of your **body changing** from that of a child into that of an adult. This happens because hormones (small chemical signals) get released into your blood and tell your body it's time to start developing. It's hard to see the changes day to day, but you may look back at a picture and be surprised how much you have developed in a short span of time!

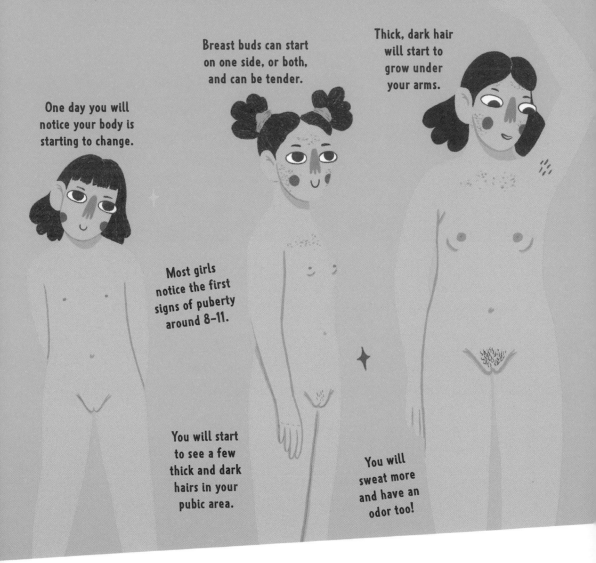

Breast buds can start on one side, or both, and can be tender.

Thick, dark hair will start to grow under your arms.

One day you will notice your body is starting to change.

Most girls notice the first signs of puberty around 8–11.

You will start to see a few thick and dark hairs in your pubic area.

You will sweat more and have an odor too!

HoW WE

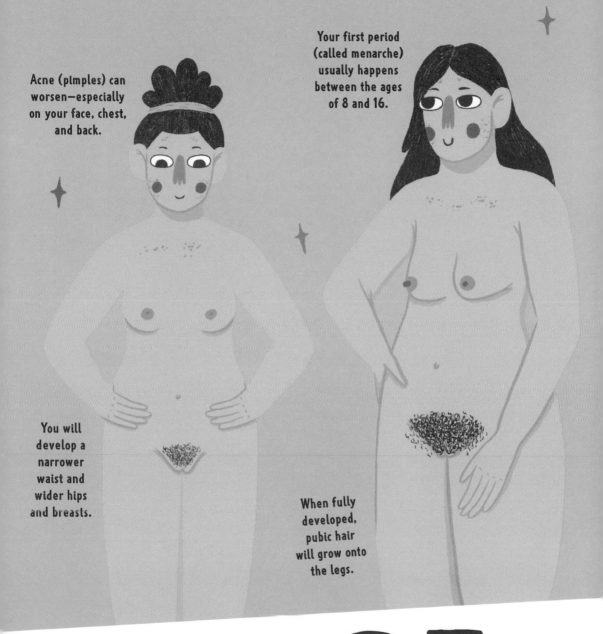

Acne (pimples) can worsen—especially on your face, chest, and back.

Your first period (called menarche) usually happens between the ages of 8 and 16.

You will develop a narrower waist and wider hips and breasts.

When fully developed, pubic hair will grow onto the legs.

CHANGE

All of the organs in your body have a purpose. Your heart pumps blood, your lungs bring in oxygen so you can breathe, and your intestines absorb nutrients from your food. Your vagina has many roles. Mainly it is a **tunnel** that allows things to go in or go out of your body. The vagina belongs to the **reproductive system**. The organs in the reproductive system include the ovaries, uterus, vulva, and vagina. These organs help us have babies (reproduce). Some of the tasks the vagina has are to help sperm get into the uterus, to **drain blood** from the uterus during a period, and to allow the passage of a baby out of your body.

After fertilization, the cells of the embryo start to **divide**.

The **fallopian tube** picks up the released egg.

Fertilized embryo

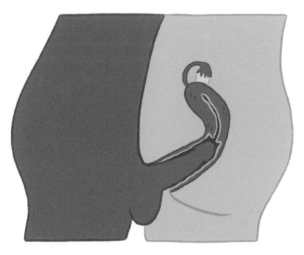

PENIS/VAGINA SEX

During penis/vagina sex, a penis is inserted into the vagina, where it releases a special fluid called semen. This fluid contains millions (yes, millions!) of reproductive cells called sperm. They look like tadpoles and swim up the vagina, through the cervix, into the uterus, up the fallopian tube, and onto an egg.

FERTILIZATION

Sperm can combine with an egg to create an embryo (a fertilized egg)—this will become a baby! Thousands of sperm attach to the egg's outer shell. As soon as the first sperm gets in, the egg's shell prevents any other sperm from getting inside.

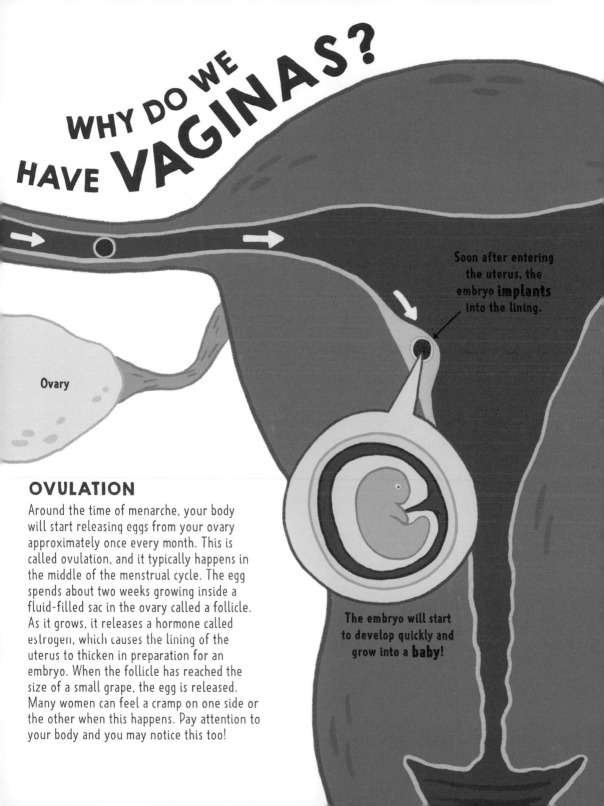

WHY DO WE HAVE VAGINAS?

Soon after entering the uterus, the embryo **implants** into the lining.

Ovary

The embryo will start to develop quickly and grow into a **baby!**

OVULATION

Around the time of menarche, your body will start releasing eggs from your ovary approximately once every month. This is called ovulation, and it typically happens in the middle of the menstrual cycle. The egg spends about two weeks growing inside a fluid-filled sac in the ovary called a follicle. As it grows, it releases a hormone called estrogen, which causes the lining of the uterus to thicken in preparation for an embryo. When the follicle has reached the size of a small grape, the egg is released. Many women can feel a cramp on one side or the other when this happens. Pay attention to your body and you may notice this too!

FIRST TRIMESTER

The fetus (unborn baby) develops all of its organs in the first ten weeks! It receives nutrients to grow through its umbilical cord, which is connected to the uterus via the placenta.

SECOND TRIMESTER

The fetus is surrounded by fluid that comes from its own pee! Many organs start functioning, and the fetus begins hearing sounds. It starts to kick and punch the walls of the uterus, which can be felt on the outside.

THIRD TRIMESTER

Final preparations for living outside the uterus are happening. The fetus practices breathing, starts growing hair, and gains weight. It usually moves to a head-down position to get ready for delivery.

THE SUPER-S T R E T C H Y
VAGINA!

The vagina's job isn't over once an egg is fertilized. It still has to allow a baby out! But how does that work? After a baby grows for nine months, the uterus—which is a muscle—starts squeezing (contracting). This is called **labor**. These contractions are like period cramps, but much bigger, and they push the baby out. The vagina can stretch to allow a baby to pass through, which is lucky—the head of the baby is about **the size of a grapefruit!**

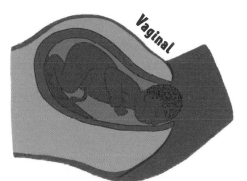
Vaginal

The vagina **stretches** to allow the baby out. It goes back to its normal size after delivery.

TYPES OF DELIVERIES

Most babies can be delivered from the vagina if they are in a head-down position. Some babies will need help getting out through a Cesarean delivery, which is surgery where the baby is removed from the abdomen. Doctors can also assist in a vaginal delivery using tools including forceps or a vacuum.

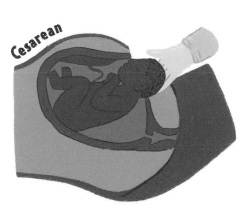
Cesarean

An **incision** (cut) is made to remove the baby from the abdomen.

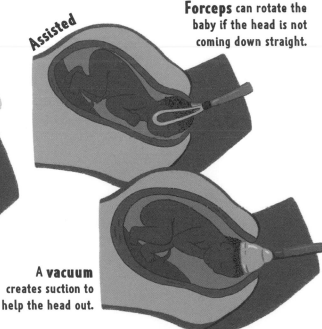
Assisted

Forceps can rotate the baby if the head is not coming down straight.

A **vacuum** creates suction to help the head out.

WHAT IS A HYMEN?

You may have heard of hymens. Over history they have been incorrectly seen as an indicator of whether or not someone has had sex. The truth? The hymen is just a **small flap of tissue** at the beginning of the vagina. Just like a vulva, it is different for everyone. Most people have a small ring of tissue, others don't have any, and some have a hymen that covers the opening to the vagina. This tissue is usually **stretched and opened** over time. Very rarely the hymen completely blocks the vagina. This is called an **imperforate hymen**, and it needs a medical procedure to open it so period blood is able to come out.

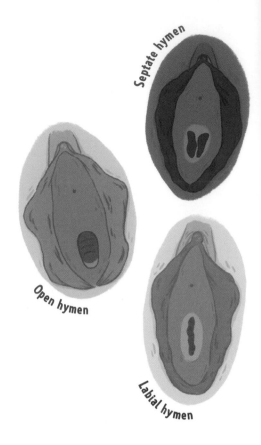

Septate hymen

Open hymen

Labial hymen

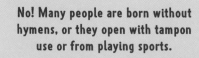

What does it mean to be a virgin?

Historically it meant never having had penetrative sex with a penis.

So if your hymen is open, does it mean you aren't a virgin?

No! Many people are born without hymens, or they open with tampon use or from playing sports.

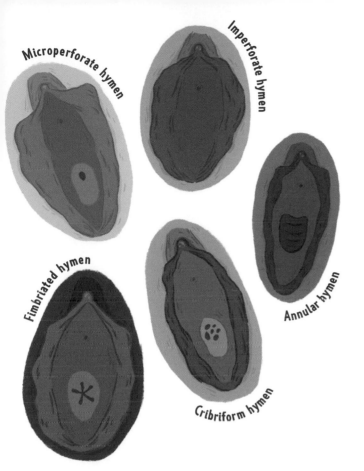

Microperforate hymen

Imperforate hymen

Fimbriated hymen

Annular hymen

Cribriform hymen

WHY DO WE HAVE THEM?

There are a lot of ideas about why we have hymens. One thought is that when we are babies they stop our vaginas from getting poop inside them. As we grow, we no longer need hymens. Often they go away on their own or are stretched during penetrative sex.

NOTHING TO DO WITH VIRGINITY

Throughout history and in different cultures, hymens have mistakenly been thought to represent virginity. No one can look at your hymen and tell what you have or have not had inside your vagina.

Also, you don't need a penis to have sex. Get with the times, people!

23

WHY DO WE GET PERIODS?

Once you hit puberty, you'll start to bleed every month— *um, WHAT?* Yes, it sounds like an inconvenience, but it's actually an extremely important function. Let me explain... The lining of the uterus needs to be in **perfect sync** with an embryo for someone to get pregnant. If the lining is too old, or too thick, an embryo cannot attach to it. If the egg that gets released at ovulation is not fertilized by sperm, and no pregnancy occurs, then a period occurs to **refresh the lining** to try again the next month. This process is called the menstrual cycle. Having a period relies on various parts of your body releasing or responding to hormones.

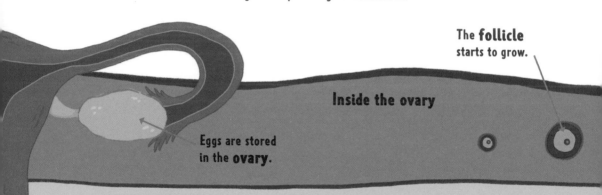

The **follicle** starts to grow.

Inside the ovary

Eggs are stored in the **ovary**.

HOW DOES YOUR BODY KNOW WHEN TO BLEED?

The pituitary gland in your brain sends a hormone signal to your ovary telling it to grow an egg. The egg is inside a sac called a follicle. As the follicle grows, it releases the hormone estrogen. This tells the uterus to grow a thick lining to prepare for an embryo. When estrogen levels are high, the egg is released, and the follicle starts producing a new hormone called progesterone. If no pregnancy occurs, both estrogen and progesterone drop, signaling to the uterus that there is no baby and it's time to have a period.

Inside the uterus

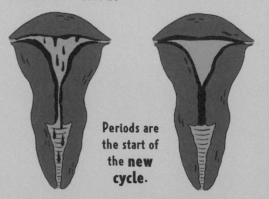

Periods are the start of the **new cycle**.

Irregular menstrual cycles can be normal for the first few years. Not ovulating is a common cause of not getting your periods. This can happen if you put stress on your body from too much weight, a loss of weight, excessive exercising, or other medical problems. If you suddenly stop getting your periods when they were previously regular, check to see if you are pregnant, and see a doctor.

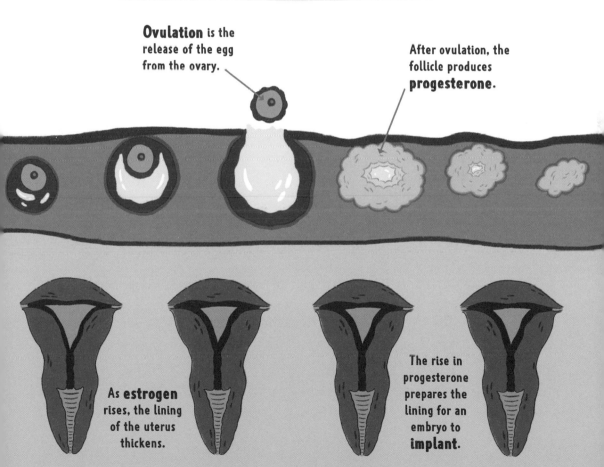

Ovulation is the release of the egg from the ovary.

After ovulation, the follicle produces **progesterone**.

As **estrogen** rises, the lining of the uterus thickens.

The rise in progesterone prepares the lining for an embryo to **implant**.

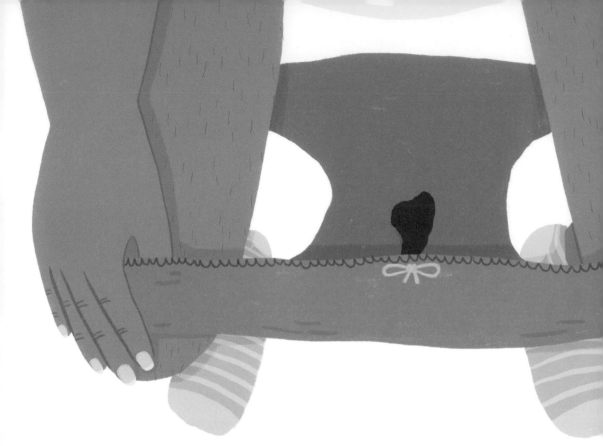

YOUR FIRST
PERIOD

THINGS TO EXPECT

You will start to notice changes in your body, from mood swings to vaginal discharge (see pages 42–43). These are caused by changing hormones. Your periods typically start two to three years after you first notice changes to your body.

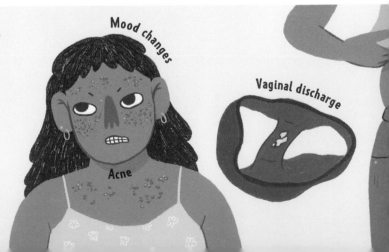

Mood changes

Vaginal discharge

Acne

Your first period will probably startle you because you will notice there is **blood in your underwear**. It's normal to have a lot of emotions about this important milestone. It can be both exciting and scary. Some people will experience increased acne, cramps, or breast tenderness in the days or weeks before their first period. The **rise and fall of hormones** can also cause some irritability and food cravings, and make you tired.

Spare underwear

Pads

Leggings or comfy pants

TOOL KIT

To prepare, keep a "period kit" in your school backpack or bag. This should contain all of the tools you will need, because periods often come unexpectedly. You will need a change of leggings or pants, clean underwear, and sanitary pads. Long before you start your periods, buy pads to have at home and practice putting them on.

Growth spurts

Tender breasts

Pelvic cramps

Pubic hair growth

PADS

Panty liners are small. They are good for very light days or spotting.

MOST PEOPLE START USING PADS WITH THEIR FIRST PERIOD.

Pads with wings are good for sleeping in and for those with heavier flows.

PERIOD CARE

Now you know what a period is, it's time to discuss what to do when you have your first period. Luckily there are lots of options. Getting comfortable with your body will help you find products that you like. You should not feel **pressured** to try different things. Some people use sanitary pads their whole lives, while others prefer tampons. What you decide to use is **up to you**. Try different ones to see what you like best!

Tampons are small cotton items with a string that are worn inside the vagina.

TAMPONS

Tampons can absorb fluid for up to 8 hours.

Some have an applicator that helps you push the tampon into your vagina.

Silicone cups are worn inside your vagina and collect fluid for up to 12 hours.

MENSTRUAL CUP

Because they are reusable, they create less waste for the environment.

MENSTRUAL UNDERWEAR

These absorbent underwear catch your blood, then you wash them.

Tampons and menstrual cups are worn inside your vagina. It takes practice to insert them, but when they are in the right place, you can't feel them at all. They are great for sports and swimming.

USING A CUP

1 The soft cup needs to be folded before it's inserted. It will unfold itself once it's inside your vagina.

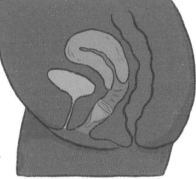

2 The cup sits in your vaginal passage. You use your fingers to grasp and remove the cup. You should empty and clean it every day.

USING A TAMPON

1 Hold the tampon by the base and slowly slide it into your vagina. The string will hang out of you.

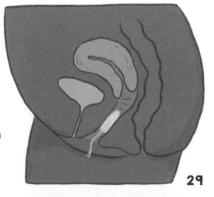

2 To remove the tampon, pull the string and put the tampon in the garbage. Never flush it down the toilet!

NO NEED TO FEEL
EMBARRASSED!

Getting your first period is an exciting milestone. While it seems very different from other milestones, like your first tooth and first steps, this is another important first! It can feel private, **uncomfortable**, and embarrassing to talk about. But remember, if you have a parent or caregiver who has had a uterus, they will have **experienced this themselves**.

HOW TO TALK ABOUT IT

While a conversation is often best, if you don't feel comfortable talking, you can consider another method of communication to share the news. You could also ask to go to the store to purchase some "sanitary products." Adults in your life will know what this means!

Send an email

Send a text or make a phone call

TRUSTED ADULT

It's a good idea to identify a trusted adult in your life to be able to ask questions. This does not need to be a parent or caregiver. It could be a sister, teacher, school nurse, aunt, cousin, or a friend's parent—someone you feel comfortable talking to.

CRAMPS!

A **hot-water bottle** or heating pad can often help.

Cramp is a type of pain that affects muscles—you may have experienced it while playing sports (it's not fun). The uterus is a **strong muscle** that contracts hard every menstrual cycle to get out the old lining to make room for a new lining. Just like other muscles in your body, when the uterus works hard, **lactic acid** builds up. This can cause pain in the form of cramps. Usually, the pain is in your lower abdomen, but sometimes you can feel it in your back or your legs. Cramps typically start at the beginning of your period and can be worse in your **teenage years**.

THINGS TO MAKE YOU FEEL BETTER

When you get cramps, you may feel like curling up in a ball. Luckily there are some tricks that can make you feel better! You need to try different techniques to see what works for your body and brings relief. Cramps should not wake you from your sleep or prevent you from doing your usual activities, such as school or sports. If they do, consider seeing your doctor.

Massage your **lower abdomen** (over the uterus) or your back when cramps are intense.

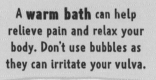

A **warm bath** can help relieve pain and relax your body. Don't use bubbles as they can irritate your vulva.

Your mind/body connection is a powerful tool! **Yoga** or **meditation** can help calm and relax you.

MEDICAL HELP

Doctors recommend two types of medication for cramps: anti-inflammatory (such as ibuprofen) and hormonal. Hormonal options (such as contraceptive pills) reduce the thickness of your uterine lining, which reduces pain.

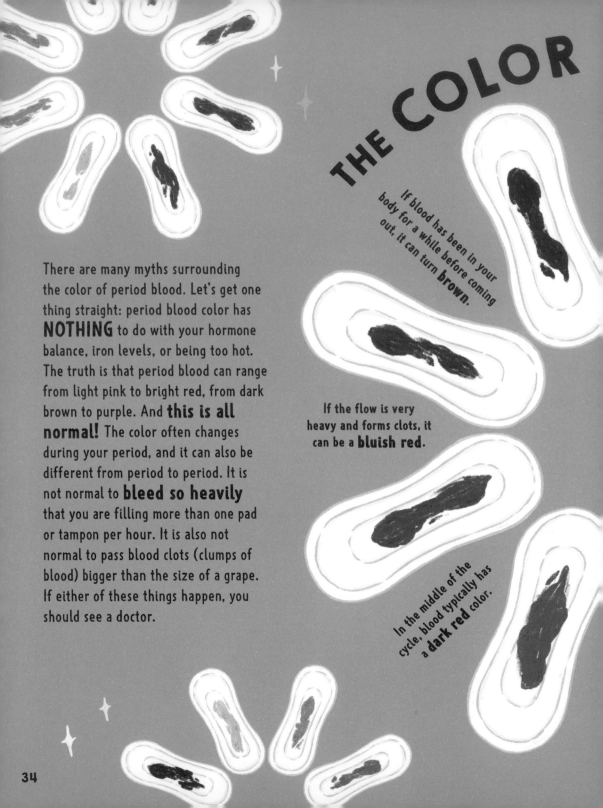

THE COLOR

If blood has been in your body for a while before coming out, it can turn **brown**.

There are many myths surrounding the color of period blood. Let's get one thing straight: period blood color has **NOTHING** to do with your hormone balance, iron levels, or being too hot. The truth is that period blood can range from light pink to bright red, from dark brown to purple. And **this is all normal!** The color often changes during your period, and it can also be different from period to period. It is not normal to **bleed so heavily** that you are filling more than one pad or tampon per hour. It is also not normal to pass blood clots (clumps of blood) bigger than the size of a grape. If either of these things happen, you should see a doctor.

If the flow is very heavy and forms clots, it can be a **bluish red**.

In the middle of the cycle, blood typically has a **dark red** color.

OF **BLOOD**

As blood mixes with white vaginal discharge, it will look **light pink**.

As more blood and less discharge are mixing, the blood becomes a **darker pink**.

Fresh bleeding that comes straight from the uterus is usually **bright red**.

CONSISTENCY

Different parts of your cycle will have different types of menstrual flow. The first few days of bleeding il might be thin, watery, or even jelly-like. The second and third days can be the heaviest days. Some people have clots or thick blood. At the end of the period, it's normal to have more stringy blood.

Thin and watery   Clots and thick   Stringy

KEEPING
CLEAN

Most people need to clean their bodies every day or two. As we grow, our **natural sweat** and residue from using the bathroom (eww) can create a smell. This odor comes from bacteria that live on our bodies. Soap and water can kill and wash away these bacteria. Like any part of your body, your vulva needs to be cleaned regularly. But remember—this is a **very sensitive** part of your body, so the way you treat it is a little different from everywhere else.

THE VAGINA DOES NOT NEED TO BE CLEANED.

LEAVE YOUR VAGINA ALONE!

The actual vagina, the inside part, SHOULD NOT be cleaned. It is actually self-cleaning (see pages 42–43). The vagina has its own healthy bacteria called lactobacilli. These bacteria keep the vagina healthy, and inserting soap can disrupt this delicate balance.

ARE YOU WIPING THE RIGHT WAY?

Yes, there is a right way to wipe after you've gone to the bathroom! It is ALWAYS front to back—whether you've done a number one or a number two. This is because the anus, where poop comes out, has a lot of bacteria that could cause irritation and infection if it got into the vagina.

Never use the same wad of toilet paper twice.

HOW TO CLEAN YOUR VULVA

You should clean the vulva while in the shower or bath using sensitive soap and water. You should get between the folds on the outside, but soap should never go on the inside. You should also clean the perineum (the skin between the vagina and the anus) and the anus itself.

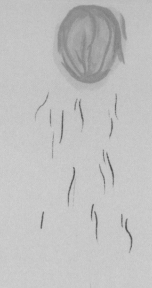

GETTING TO KNOW YOUR
KNOW YOUR
PUBES

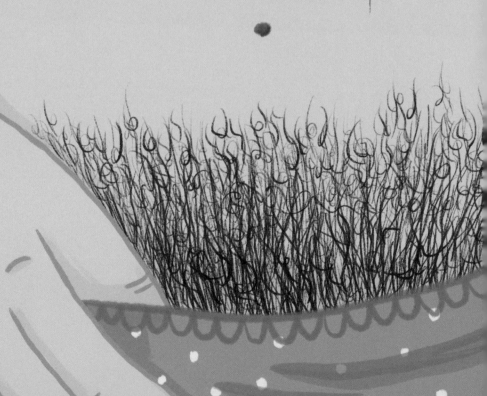

Pubic hair might be somewhat of a surprise when it first appears, but it plays several important roles. Pubes protect delicate labia from rubbing against clothes—especially for people who have larger labia minora that hang down. They also provide a barrier that **protects the vagina** from germs, debris, and dirt. For many people, pubic hair will grow down onto their legs. You can decide if you want to groom your pubic hair, or let it **grow naturally** into a nice big bush! If you have thick, dark, coarse hair in places that seem abnormal (such as your back, chest, or face) then it might be worth seeing a doctor to check your hormone levels.

INGROWN HAIRS

Removing your pubic hair can cause ingrown hairs. If pubic hair is curly and you cut it below the skin, it can grow back under the skin. This can cause painful bumps, irritation, and sometimes infection. A safe way to remove pubic hair is to use scissors to trim the hair (being careful not to cut yourself).

The best way to avoid ingrown hairs is to remove hair **above the skin**.

Waxing traps hair in wax, which is **ripped off** to pull the hair out. OUCH!

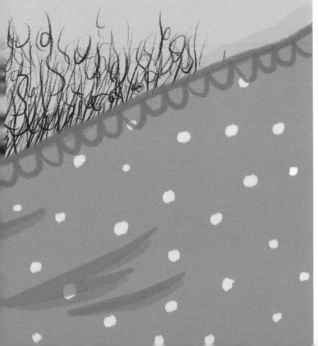

SEEING A
GYNECOLOGIST

A gynecologist is a doctor who specializes in the female reproductive organs. Unless there is a problem, typically these visits do not include an examination—just a conversation! Gynecologists are there to be **reliable sources** of medical information. You should be able to have a private conversation with your doctor **without your parents or caregivers** in the room. It can seem overwhelming or embarrassing, but here are a few of the kinds of things they will want to talk to you about.

HOW OFTEN ARE YOU GETTING YOUR PERIODS?

It's normal for periods to be irregular in the first few years of getting them. Your doctor can make sure it hasn't been too long since you've had a period. If it has, they can recommend things that could help, such as ways to track your periods.

ARE YOUR PERIODS TOO HEAVY OR TOO PAINFUL?

You shouldn't have to suffer with your periods. If you bleed too much, your doctor will be able to help. If you have bad cramps, your gynecologist can prescribe medication.

CHECKING YOUR PUBERTY IS ON TRACK

Although everyone develops at a different rate, your doctor will want to know how your puberty is progressing—with starting your periods, your pubic hair growing, and your breasts developing.

PAP SMEAR

A pap smear, or pap test, is a routine medical examination. It checks for changes that can suggest an increased risk of cervical cancer in people with a cervix. Cervical cancer is a type of cancer that is typically caused by a sexually transmitted infection called human papillomavirus (HPV). During a pap smear, a doctor will gently remove a few cells from your cervix with a brush and a spatula. Lots of people get nervous about getting a pap smear, but they aren't scary, only last a couple of minutes, and are very important! Usually you have your first pap smear when you're in your twenties.

DISCUSSING HEALTHY RELATIONSHIPS

You should not feel pressured or forced into sexual activity (see pages 50–53). You deserve to be with a partner who is respectful and understanding, and does not harm you emotionally or physically. These are issues you can talk through with your doctor.

EDUCATING YOU ABOUT OPTIONS TO PREVENT PREGNANCY

It's important that you understand what you need to do to prevent pregnancy until you are ready to start a family. Your doctor can educate you and prescribe birth control.

INFORMING YOU ABOUT SEXUALLY TRANSMITTED INFECTIONS

Infections can be spread by having sex. Condoms are the best way to prevent sexually transmitted infections (STIs). Doctors can check to see if you have any STIs and will be able to treat some infections. Unfortunately not all STIs can be treated.

THE SELF-CLEANING VAGINA!

Did you know that your vagina is **self-cleaning**? That's right! It produces something called discharge. This is a **white fluid** that you might have noticed in your underwear before. Discharge is an important fluid that your vagina uses to clean and lubricate itself. It protects your vagina and other reproductive organs against **unwanted bacteria**. It also helps keep the vagina lubricated for sexual intercourse, so that it is not painful. Discharge is normal and super important for keeping your **vagina healthy** (and who doesn't want a healthy vagina?).

NOTICING DISCHARGE FOR THE FIRST TIME

You will first notice discharge about 6-12 months before you start your periods. You'll spot a white crust or fluid on your underwear, which is not pee! Don't panic—this is totally normal.

TYPES OF DISCHARGE

Your discharge changes throughout the menstrual cycle. As the egg starts to grow, the discharge becomes stretchy and wet, which allows sperm to get in more easily. After you ovulate, the discharge becomes dry and sticky.

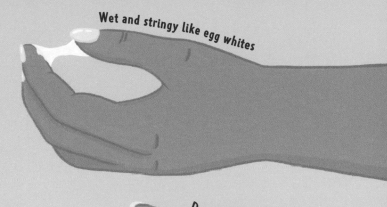

Wet and stringy like egg whites

Dry and sticky like glue

BECAUSE DISCHARGE IS ACIDIC, IT CAN **STAIN** OR **BLEACH** YOUR UNDERWEAR.

WATCH OUT FOR CHANGES

If your discharge develops a strong odor or turns a different color, you may have an infection and should see a doctor. Here are what different types of discharge mean:

Pink discharge may be normal discharge mixed with a small drop of period blood.

Discharge with a bad smell might indicate an infection.

White, clear, or yellowish discharge is normal.

Very thick, chunky discharge may be a sign of a yeast infection.

Green or gray discharge may be a sign of infection.

Do you ever feel the need to **scratch** downstairs? You're not alone! The vagina and vulva are very sensitive. If irritated, they can become itchy. The vulva is a wet and warm place that makes it susceptible to infection, allergy, and irritation. The cause of the itchiness may be what we call **contact dermatitis**, which is irritation from soap or detergent used on your clothes or skin. It can also be the result of damage caused by clothes, fingers, sexual activity, or even **wiping too hard** after going to the bathroom. It can also be the result of an infection or a skin disorder. But don't worry—there are plenty of things you can do to relieve the need to itch!

ITCHY VULVAS

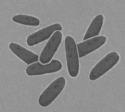

Did you know there is GOOD bacteria? Your vagina is home to millions of healthy bacteria called lactobacilli that protect your body from harmful bacteria that can cause problems.

Heat and **moisture** increase irritation, so sleeping without any underwear on can get more air to your vulva.

THINGS TO HELP

Keeping your vulva clean and avoiding anything that can cause irritation will help you feel better quickly. Try to avoid scratching, since this can cause more damage to the delicate skin of your vulva. Here are a few things that may help to reduce the itchiness you're experiencing.

Use **non-perfumed soaps** that are made for sensitive skin.

Wear cotton underwear. Cotton is a fabric that **absorbs moisture** and allows air in.

Pee and poop can irritate the skin. Make sure to always wipe from **front to back** to protect your vulva.

Take a cool or **lukewarm bath** (not too hot), and add ¼ cup (32 g) of baking soda. This will help combat any acidic infections.

WHAT'S IT SUPPOSED TO SMELL

Your vulva should not smell **strong** or **fishy**. This could be the sign of an infection.

Lots of people like to talk about what vulvas should and shouldn't smell like. Some companies make **a lot of money** by trying to convince people that their natural smell is wrong, dirty, and needs to be covered and washed away. The truth? Each vulva has its own smell—and this is completely normal! Everyone's smell is a little bit different, but it is healthy to have a **light odor**. Of course, good hygiene is always important. You should try to shower frequently—especially if you are sweaty, have been swimming, or are on your period.

LIKE DOWN THERE?

Despite what people say, your vulva shouldn't smell like **flowers** or **pineapples!**

You do not need special soap, sprays, or douches for your vulva.

DON'T BE ASHAMED OF YOUR SMELL. YOUR VULVA IS SUPPOSED TO SMELL LIKE... A VULVA!

GENDER IDENTITY

How do you know who you are, who you want to be, and who you are attracted to? For some people this comes easily, but for others it takes some time, exploration, and **learning about yourself**—and that's OK! When you were born, doctors looked between your legs and assigned your sex. If that is the end of the story for you, great. But if that assignment doesn't **fit properly**, you are the only one who can figure out what is right. People in your life may have expectations of who they want you to be. You need to be only one person: your true, authentic self.

CISGENDER

When your gender identity matches your assigned sex, you are cisgender. Cisgender means identifying as male if you were assigned male or identifying as female if you were assigned female. It is important to know this has nothing to do with your gender expression or your sexual orientation (if you are attracted to males, females, both, or neither).

GENDER IDENTITY

Your gender identity is your personal feeling of your own gender. It does not need to be the same as your assigned sex. It also does not need to be the same as your gender expression—how masculine or feminine you decide to appear or behave. It's how you FEEL about yourself. The only person who can determine your gender identity is you. This can take time to figure out as you explore and get to know yourself better.

NONBINARY

Nonbinary means that you do not identify as only male or only female. Some people identify along the spectrum between them. There are several terms you may hear that are associated with being nonbinary, including gender neutral, gender queer, gender fluid, gender diverse, and gender nonconforming. People who identify as nonbinary can use pronouns like they/them, but may chose to use more binary pronouns (she/her and he/him). It depends on what makes them most comfortable!

TRANSGENDER

When your gender identity and gender expression are different from your assigned sex, you may be described as transgender, or trans. Some trans people express their gender with their hair, clothing, by using a new name, and by using pronouns of their preferred gender, but never physically change their body. Other trans people use hormonal treatments and sometimes surgery to permanently change their body to be more aligned with their gender identity.

GENDER DYSPHORIA

People who are transgender can feel trapped in the wrong body. This feeling is often referred to as gender dysphoria. It can cause significant anxiety and depression. There are doctors and clinics that specialize in treating gender dysphoria. It's very important to take care of your mental health—remember you aren't alone!

STAYING SAFE

As your body is changing, you will develop new feelings and emotions. You might start **dating** (we'd need a whole other book just about that!) and, along the way, you could decide to send your partner nude photos or videos of yourself. It may seem fun, flirty, or innocent at the time, but a lot can go wrong. Images can **easily be shared** and make their way to the wrong people. Even a temporary or private image can be saved with a screenshot. It's important to be **smart** and careful—don't take naked pictures of yourself.

IF SOMEONE RESPECTS YOU, THEY WILL NOT ASK YOU TO SEND THEM A PICTURE OF YOURSELF NAKED.

BEST COURSE OF ACTION

If you have sent a nude text, what can you do to protect yourself? Truthfully, not much. The first thing to do is to delete any naked images or texts and ask your partner to delete them too. If someone tries to convince you to send a nude text, tell them it makes you feel uncomfortable and refuse to do it.

Where's that pic I asked for?

•••

I don't think I can send it. I don't feel comfortable, and it could end up getting shared. It's just too risky.

•••

THINK CAREFULLY

Sexually explicit texts (sexts) are illegal if you are under 18. If you are under that age you should never take a picture of yourself or anyone else naked. Even if you trust your partner, things can change. You might break up, someone else may look at your phone, or someone could share the picture. Even if you delete a photo from your phone, it might be stored somewhere else. Never share someone else's sext. This is cruel, illegal, and can cause serious emotional harm. It may seem a long way off now, but sexting may also harm your future educational or job prospects.

TALK TO AN ADULT AND REPORT IT

What should you do if someone sends you a sext? First, do not share or forward it. This is illegal and the photo can can end up in the wrong place. If you feel pressured or bullied, do not delete the message until you have told a trusted adult. They will be able to advise you on how to report the sext to the relevant authorities.

NO MEANS NO

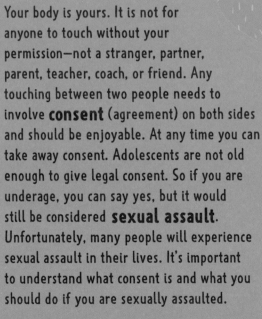

Your body is yours. It is not for anyone to touch without your permission—not a stranger, partner, parent, teacher, coach, or friend. Any touching between two people needs to involve **consent** (agreement) on both sides and should be enjoyable. At any time you can take away consent. Adolescents are not old enough to give legal consent. So if you are underage, you can say yes, but it would still be considered **sexual assault**. Unfortunately, many people will experience sexual assault in their lives. It's important to understand what consent is and what you should do if you are sexually assaulted.

WHEN CAN CONSENT BE GIVEN?

If someone has not agreed to something—either through their **words** or their **body language**—no consent has been given.

Consent can be **withdrawn** at any time. If someone changes their mind and wants to stop, consent has been taken away.

Consent can't be given if someone has had **too much alcohol** to drink and can't make clear decisions.

Consent can't be given if someone is **asleep** or **passed out**.

Consent involves continuously getting **permission** from a partner by asking questions like: *is this OK? Do you like this? Should we continue?*

WHAT TO DO IF YOU ARE SEXUALLY ASSAULTED

If you have been sexually assaulted, you should immediately seek medical attention to get protected against STIs and pregnancy. Get somewhere safe and go to a hospital as soon as possible. Remember, it is not your fault and there are professionals who will be able to support you.

UNDERSTANDING THE RISKS

When you're old enough, you and a partner may want to have sex. Above all, sex is supposed to be **fun!** However, it is important to understand the risks of being **sexually active**, so you can prepare properly. The two main risks involve unwanted pregnancy and sexually transmitted infections (STIs). The only method that prevents both pregnancy and STIs is using condoms, but even these aren't 100% effective. These pages outline some of the other forms of **contraception** you can consider using. Some of these you can buy from a store. Others need to be prescribed by a doctor.

A male condom is a rubber cover that is put onto a penis during sexual activity and stops **semen** (cum) from entering the vagina.

MALE CONDOM

IMPLANT
This small implant goes **under the skin** on your arm and stops ovulation for three years.

FEMALE CONDOM
A female condom is placed into the vagina. An **external ring** sits on the vulva and prevents exposure to sperm.

SPERM CAN LIVE FOR FIVE DAYS INSIDE YOU!

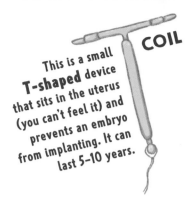

COIL

This is a small **T-shaped** device that sits in the uterus (you can't feel it) and prevents an embryo from implanting. It can last 5–10 years.

PILLS

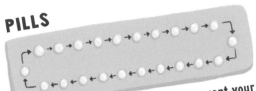

Some hormonal pills can prevent your body from releasing an egg and **stop implantation** into the uterus.

INJECTION

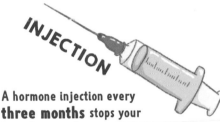

A hormone injection every **three months** stops your body from ovulating and prevents implantation into the uterus.

MORNING-AFTER PILL

If a condom breaks during sex or you had an unplanned exposure to sperm, you can take the morning after pill. This prevents pregnancy. Take it **as soon as possible**.

BE SMART!

Any type of sexual activity, even once, can result in an infection. Vaginal secretions, semen, and saliva can all contain a variety of bacteria and viruses that can make you sick. Some of these infections have no cure—which is why it's so important to practice safe sex. If you have a vagina and are only sexually active with someone else with a vagina, you still can get an STI. If you think you may have contracted an STI, then please see a medical provider to get treatment. Treat infections as soon as they start to prevent long-term effects.

TOUCHING YOURSELF

Exploring your body is an important part of understanding it. Touching yourself for sexual arousal is called **masturbation**. There are a lot of myths out there about masturbating, but it is a normal thing to do and does not cause any harm. Touching your vulva, clitoris, or even your nipples or anus can lead to a pleasurable sensation called an **orgasm**. When you orgasm, it causes the vaginal and pelvic floor muscles to contract. The more you can understand what feels good, and what doesn't, the more you will be able to enjoy it.

MYTH BUSTING

There are many myths about touching yourself that are simply not true. Masturbating is not bad for you. It will not make you go blind, cause infertility, or make you grow hair on your palms!

BENEFITS

Touching yourself is the safest form of arousal. There is no risk of sexually transmitted infections. It is not dirty or weird, but normal! It is also normal if you don't masturbate or have orgasms. After an orgasm, the pituitary gland in your brain releases a hormone called oxytocin. This hormone causes a feeling of relaxation, calm, and bonding. It can even help with menstrual cramps.

YOUR BODY IS
AMAZING

If this book has taught you one thing, hopefully it's that, as a proud owner of a vagina, you rock. You are a walking **superhuman**. Your vagina can stretch to fit a whole new human. It can clean itself. You have, or will have, awesome pubes that protect your vulva from rubbing against clothes! Let's continue to break the negative perception of vaginas.

This book **does not cover everything**. So if you aren't sure about something, talk to a trusted adult or see your doctor. And a few reminders:

- Keep yourself safe. Protect yourself from pregnancy before you are ready, and beware of sexually transmitted infections.
- Trust yourself. If something doesn't feel right, go with your gut.

- You will make mistakes along the way. Learning from them is the key to being your best self.
- Be kind to yourself. You aren't perfect, and that's OK. You deserve to be loved and celebrated for exactly who you are.

Growing from a child to an adult is a difficult journey. As your body is changing, it will take some practice to get used to taking care of it. **Empower yourself** with knowledge about your health.

And last of all, don't forget: **We need to talk about vaginas!** You should be proud to share knowledge about your body and health.

GLOSSARY

CONDOM
A cover put on a penis to prevent semen from entering another person's body.

CONSENT
When two or more people agree on something. Consent must be given before any sexual activity occurs.

CRAMPS
Muscle pains, which can be caused by periods. People can feel period cramps in their stomach, back, or legs.

DISCHARGE
A fluid produced by the vagina to clean and lubricate itself.

FETUS
An unborn baby inside the womb.

GENDER IDENTITY
A person's feelings about their gender.

GYNECOLOGIST
A doctor who specializes in the female reproductive organs.

HORMONES
Special chemicals released by your body that can affect your mood, appetite, and growth.

HYMEN
A thin flap of tissue at the vaginal opening.

INGROWN HAIRS
Hair that grows under the skin.

LABIA
The inner and outer skin folds (or lips) that surround the vagina. Part of the vulva.

LACTOBACILLI
Healthy bacteria inside the vagina.

MASTURBATION
The act of touching oneself for sexual pleasure.

MENSTRUAL CUP
A reusable silicone cup worn inside the vagina that collects period blood.

NONBINARY
A person who doesn't identify as only male or only female.

ORGASM

A pleasurable peak of sensation that occurs while being intimate or masturbating.

OVARIES

The organ in a woman's body where eggs are stored, connected to the uterus (womb).

OVULATION

When an egg is released from the ovary during the menstrual cycle.

PAP SMEAR

A medical examination to check for signs of cervical cancer.

PERIOD

Also called menstruation, a period is bleeding caused by the uterus shedding its lining each month.

PUBERTY

The process your body goes through when you are transitioning from a child to an adult.

PUBIC HAIR

Hair that grows around sexual organs and protects them against germs.

SEMEN

A fluid containing sperm, which is released by a penis during sexual activity.

SEXT

A text message of a sexual nature. Sexually explicit texts are illegal if you are under 18.

SEXUALLY TRANSMITTED INFECTION (STI)

An infection that is passed on during sexual activity.

SPERM

Reproductive cells in semen. When sperm combines with an egg it creates an embryo, which will become a baby.

TAMPON

A cotton period product worn inside the vagina to absorb blood.

UTERUS

Also called the womb, the uterus is the organ inside a woman's body where babies develop and grow.

VULVA

All the external parts of your genitals.

INDEX